THE MAN WHO SAID THANK YOU

Ella K. Lindvall

© 1982, 1994 by
THE MOODY BIBLE INSTITUTE
OF CHICAGO

This story has been extracted from
Read-Aloud Bible Stories, vol. 1

Illustrated by
H. Kent Puckett

Printed in Mexico

MOODY PRESS

One, two, three,
four, five, six,
seven, eight, nine,
ten men were very sick.
They were so sick
the doctor couldn't
make them better.

They were so sick
they couldn't stay
with their mommies
and daddies or
boys and girls.
They had to stay outside
by themselves.

All of them
wanted to be well
so they could go home.

One day
the ten sick men saw
lots of people
coming up the road.

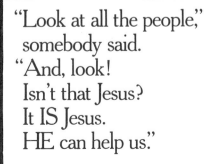

"Look at all the people,"
somebody said.
"And, look!
Isn't that Jesus?
It IS Jesus.
HE can help us."

Jesus was far away, so the men yelled in big voices, "JESUS, HELP US! JESUS, HELP US!"

Now, Jesus knows everything.
He knew what they wanted.
Right away,
He called back,

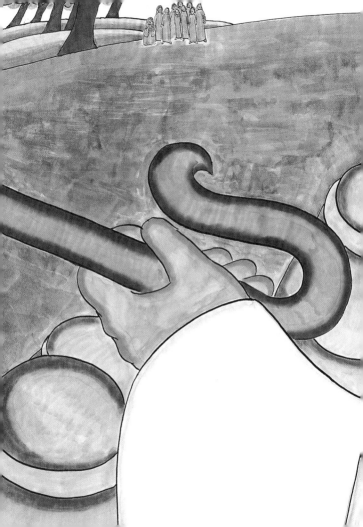

"Go to the men
who work in
God's Temple-church.
Let them see if
you are still sick."

I'm glad to tell you
the men did just what
Jesus said.
One, two, three,
four, five, six,
seven, eight, nine,
ten sick men started
down the road.
Step, step, step.
Step, step, step.

All at once
somebody said,
"Oh, my hands—they're better!"
Another man said,
"My arms—they're better!"

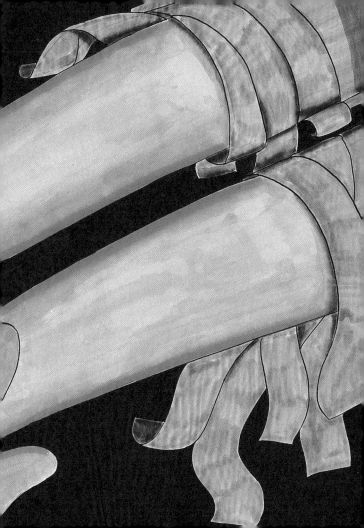

Somebody else shouted,
"Jesus has made us well.
NOW WE CAN GO HOME."
And away they hurried—
one, two, three,
four, five, six,
seven, eight, nine men.
Just nine.

One man didn't
hurry home.
That man wanted
to say, "Thank You,"
first.
He ran back to Jesus.

"Thank God!"
the man shouted.
"I'm well!
Thank You,"
he said to Jesus.
"Thank You.
Thank You."

Jesus was pleased.
But He was sad, too.
"Didn't I make
ten men well?" He asked.
"Did only one man
come back to say, 'Thank You'?"
Then He told the man
he could go home.

What did you learn?

Jesus was pleased
when the man
thanked Him.
Jesus is pleased
when YOU tell Him,
"Thank You."
What could you
thank Jesus for
right now?

About the Author

Ella K. Lindvall (A.B., Taylor
University; Wheaton College;
Northern Illinois University) is a
mother and former elementary
school teacher. She is the author
of *The Bible Illustrated for Little
Children*, and *Read-Aloud Bible
Stories*, volumes I, II, III, and IV.